Shall We Dance?
HIP-HOP DANCE

by Wendy Hinote Lanier

FOCUS READERS

www.focusreaders.com

Focus Readers is distributed by North Star Editions:
sales@northstareditions.com | 888-417-0195

Produced for Focus Readers by Red Line Editorial.

Photographs ©: Mlenny/iStockphoto, cover, 1; ginosphotos/iStockphoto, 4–5; PYMCAUIG Universal Images Group/Newscom, 7; Creatista/iStockphoto, 9; ra2studio/Shutterstock Images, 10–11; oneinchpunch/iStockphoto, 13; blanaru/iStockphoto, 14–15, 29; jonya/iStockphoto, 17; Benis Arapovic/iStockphoto, 18; szefei/Shutterstock Images, 21; LarsZahnerPhotography/iStockphoto, 22–23; Polka Dot Images/iStockphoto, 25; Pavel L Photo and Video/Shutterstock Images, 26

ISBN
978-1-63517-274-4 (hardcover)
978-1-63517-339-0 (paperback)
978-1-63517-469-4 (ebook pdf)
978-1-63517-404-5 (hosted ebook)

Library of Congress Control Number: 2017935122

Printed in the United States of America
Mankato, MN
June, 2017

About the Author

Wendy Hinote Lanier is a native Texan and former elementary teacher who writes and speaks for children and adults on a variety of topics. She is the author of more than 20 books for children and young people. Some of her favorite people are dogs.

TABLE OF CONTENTS

CHAPTER 1

WHAT IS HIP-HOP DANCE?

The street party begins. It's time to dance. Hip-hop is an athletic style of street dance. Dancers might pop or lock. They might spin on their heads or backs. Break dancing moves are common, too.

Hip-hop dancers are known for their fun, energetic styles.

Hip-hop dance is part of hip-hop culture. The culture includes music and art, too. Hip-hop began in the 1970s. It started in the Bronx in New York City. Neighborhoods there hosted block parties. Usually a **DJ** hosted the event. Clive Campbell was one of them. He and his sister

DANCE TIP

You need good upper-body strength to break-dance. Increase upper-body strength by doing push-ups or working with a weighted ball.

 Clive Campbell was nicknamed DJ Kool Herc.

hosted a block party in the summer
of 1973. Their goal was to raise
money to buy new school clothes.

Clive was only 16 years old. But his style caught on. Clive began **isolating** drum breaks in popular music. This involved two **turntables**. He switched back and forth between them. These breaks could be repeated. This gave dancers plenty of time to show off their moves.

DANCE TIP

Keep your arms and hands relaxed and loose at your sides.

 Breaking is often done in groups.

Clive's party was the birth of hip-hop. Clive was the first to call the dancers break boys, or b-boys. Their style of dancing soon became known as breaking, or break dancing.

CHAPTER 2

WHAT TO WEAR

Hip-hop dancers create their own style. Clothes usually reflect **urban** street wear. Many dancers wear sweatpants or cargo pants. Oversized T-shirts or hoodies are common. Others prefer tank tops.

A hip-hop dancer shows off her style.

The key is to dress in layers. You can cool off by removing a layer when needed.

Busting a big move can be dangerous. Safety gear helps prevent injuries. Dancers sometimes wear wrist pads, elbow pads, and knee pads.

DANCE TIP

Dance shoes should allow you to slip and spin. If the soles grip too hard, you could fall or injure yourself.

 Hip-hop dancers dress to look good and move freely.

Sneakers or soft-soled shoes work great for hip-hop. High-top sneakers are a popular choice, too. For **competitions** or **exhibitions**, you might want a special pair for dancing.

CHAPTER 3

POP AND LOCK IT

Creativity is key in hip-hop dancing. Dancers bring their own moves or style. But there are a few basic moves you'll want to master. One is called popping. First you **contract** a muscle.

Hip-hop dancers combine many different types of movements.

Then you quickly release it. Doing so causes a jerk or pop. Popping is usually combined with other moves and poses.

Locking is also common. It starts when a dancer makes a quick move. Then the dancer locks into position for a few seconds. Locking is often done to make viewers laugh.

The boogaloo is another basic move. It uses mostly the hips and legs. Dancers try to make it appear as if they have no bones.

 Break-dancers often use their hands in their moves.

Breaking is one of the best-known parts of hip-hop dance. It features fun, **acrobatic** moves. Head spins are common. So are back spins.

 A break-dancer practices a head spin.

DANCE TIP

Watch other dancers to find fresh ideas. You can try to copy their moves.

Some moves are unique to hip-hop dance. Hip-hop dancers also borrow moves from other **social** dances. They might use jazz or funk moves. Sometimes they even look to gymnastics or martial arts. These moves are combined with basic hip-hop **choreography**. This is often seen in music videos.

THE CRADLE

Any good dance needs a killer ending. A freeze move called the cradle does the trick.

1. Start by sitting with your feet tucked under your bottom. Your knees should be spread apart.
2. Press your arms together. They should touch from the wrist to the elbow.
3. Keep your elbows firmly against your stomach. Lean forward. Open your arms and place your hands on the floor.
4. Now lift yourself up onto your hands. Turn your head to the side. Now freeze!

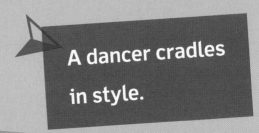

A dancer cradles in style.

CHAPTER 4

SHOW OFF WITH YOUR CREW

By the 1980s, hip-hop dance was becoming popular. It was featured in movies. Some television shows had hip-hop dancers, too. And the style continued to gain popularity.

High-energy moves make hip-hop dance fun to watch.

By the 1990s, hip-hop dance was in many music videos.

Today's hip-hop dancers often perform without a set plan. They can be creative. This is called hip-hop freestyling. It includes classic hip-hop moves. But the best freestyling includes some original moves, too.

Dance groups are called crews. Sometimes they challenge each other to friendly competitions. The competitions are called battles.

 Break-dancers must be strong to show off their most acrobatic moves.

Dance battles allow dancers to show off their best moves. Freestyling, dance crews, and battles are the main ingredients of the hip-hop style.

 Hip-hop crews practice hard to make sure their moves match when they get to competition.

Hip-hop competitions can be more than just neighborhood dance-offs. Some are featured on TV. Competitions are held all over the world. They give dance crews a chance to win money and recognition. Judges look for creative routines and flawless moves. They give each crew a score. A 10 is a perfect score.

Hip-hop dance is a great way to have fun and make new friends. And with a little practice, you could bust a move with the best of them.

DANCE TIP

Relax and have fun. Don't worry about how you look to others.

FOCUS ON
HIP-HOP DANCE

Write your answers on a separate piece of paper.

1. Write a letter to a friend explaining how hip-hop began.

2. What is your favorite hip-hop dance move? Why?

3. How does the boogaloo make dancers appear?
   - **A.** as though they are playing a trumpet
   - **B.** as though they have no bones
   - **C.** as though they are made of a stiff material

4. Why would someone want to participate in a hip-hop battle?
   - **A.** to earn the praise and respect of his or her friends
   - **B.** to convince others to dance hip-hop
   - **C.** to hear new music

5. What does **culture** mean in this book?

*Hip-hop dance is part of hip-hop **culture**. The culture includes music and art, too.*

    A. manners appropriate for a formal party

    B. a famous museum in New York City

    C. the actions and beliefs of a
       particular group

6. What does **freestyling** mean in this book?

*Today's hip-hop dancers often perform without a set plan. They can be creative. This is called hip-hop **freestyling**.*

    A. dance routines with
       no planned set
       of moves

    B. dance routines you
       need to memorize

    C. dance routines with
       all the basic moves

Answer key on page 32.

GLOSSARY

acrobatic
Showing skillful control of one's body.

choreography
The arrangement of steps and movements for a dance.

competitions
Events in which teams try to beat each other.

contract
To bring a muscle together and make it shorter.

DJ
A person who plays music for dances and parties.

exhibitions
Displays or demonstrations for the public.

isolating
Setting something apart from the rest.

social
Having to do with activities involving other people.

turntables
Machines that spin records.

urban
Relating to a city environment.

TO LEARN MORE

BOOKS

Fuhrer, Margaret. *American Dance: The Complete Illustrated History*. Minneapolis: Voyageur Press, 2014.

Garofoli, Wendy. *Hip-Hop Dancing: The Basics*. Mankato, MN: Capstone Press, 2011.

Royston, Angela. *Hip-Hop*. Chicago: Heinemann-Raintree, 2013.

NOTE TO EDUCATORS

Visit **www.focusreaders.com** to find lesson plans, activities, links, and other resources related to this title.

INDEX

Answer Key: 1. Answers will vary; **2.** Answers will vary; **3.** B; **4.** A; **5.** C; **6.** A